**MEATS** 2

# Contents

**POULTRY AND FISH** 8

**MEATLESS** 14

Copyright © Meredith Corporation 2009.
All rights reserved.
Printed in China.
ISBN 978-0-696-24343-1

**SOUPS AND STEWS** 20

# Meats

**Fork-tender meats fill this chapter to the brim. Find roasts, chops and ethnic dishes full of rich seasonings and new twists.**

Cranberry Orange
Pork Chops

*Eliminating the step of prebrowning the chops jump-starts this tasty, satisfying meal.*

# Cranberry Orange Pork Chops

**Prep:** 15 minutes  **Cook:** 7 to 8 hours on low-heat or 3½ to 4 hours on high-heat setting  **Stand:** 5 minutes
**Slow Cooker:** 3½- or 4-quart

  1 package (16 ounces) peeled baby carrots
  8 boneless pork chops, cut about ¾ inch thick (about 1¾ pounds)
  1 package (12 ounces) cranberry-orange sauce
  2 tablespoons quick-cooking tapioca
  1 teaspoon finely grated lemon zest
  ¼ teaspoon ground cardamom
  3 fresh plums and/or apricots, pitted and sliced (about 8 ounces)
    Hot cooked couscous or rice
    Chopped fresh parsley (optional)

**1.** Place carrots in a 3½- or 4-quart slow cooker. Top with pork chops.

**2.** In medium-size bowl, combine cranberry-orange sauce, tapioca, lemon zest and cardamom; pour over pork chops.

**3.** Cover slow cooker; cook on low-heat setting for 7 to 8 hours or on high-heat setting for 3½ to 4 hours. Stir in sliced fruit. Turn off slow cooker; cover and let stand for 5 minutes. Serve with hot cooked couscous or rice. If desired, sprinkle with parsley. Makes 8 servings.

**Per serving:** 323 cal., 4 g total fat (1 g sat. fat), 55 mg chol., 73 mg sodium, 47 g carbo., 3 g fiber, 22 g pro.

---

**SERVE-ALONG OPTIONS:** steamed green beans and assorted fresh berries topped with whipped cream and crushed shortbread cookies.

### Slow Cooker Smarts

*Thaw raw meat completely in the refrigerator or defrost it in the microwave before adding it to the slow cooker. If the meat thaws as it cooks, it will stay in the bacterial danger zone (40°F to 140°F) for too long.*

*Dried Japanese somen noodles have a very fine texture similar to that of angel hair pasta. Find them wrapped in bundles in Asian markets.*

# Lo Mein-Style Pork

**Prep:** 20 minutes  **Cook:** 6½ to 7 hours on low-heat or 3½ to 4 hours on high-heat setting, plus 10 to 15 minutes on high-heat setting  **Slow Cooker:** 3½- or 4-quart

  1½ pounds boneless pork shoulder
  2 cups loose-pack frozen sliced carrots
  1 jar (12 ounces) teriyaki glaze
  2 medium-size onions, cut into wedges
  1 cup thinly bias-sliced celery
  1 can (8 ounces) sliced water chestnuts, drained
  1 can (5 ounces) sliced bamboo shoots, drained
  1 teaspoon finely chopped fresh ginger
  1 package (6 ounces) frozen pea pods
  1 cup broccoli flowerets
  9 ounces somen noodles
  ½ cup cashews

**1.** Trim fat from pork. Cut pork into ¾-inch pieces. In 3½- or 4-quart slow cooker, combine pork, frozen carrots, teriyaki glaze, onions, celery, water chestnuts, bamboo shoots and ginger.

**2.** Cover slow cooker; cook on low-heat setting for 6½ to 7 hours or on high-heat setting for 3½ to 4 hours.

**3.** If necessary, raise temperature to high-heat setting. Stir frozen pea pods and broccoli into mixture in slow cooker. Cover slow cooker; cook for 10 to 15 minutes longer or until pea pods are crisp-tender.

**4.** Meanwhile, cook noodles following package directions; drain. Serve pork mixture over noodles. Sprinkle each serving with cashews. Makes 6 servings.

**Per serving:** 509 cal., 12 g total fat (3 g sat. fat), 73 mg chol., 2,274 mg sodium, 66 g carbo., 6 g fiber, 33 g pro.

---

**SERVE-ALONG OPTIONS:** purchased pot stickers and fortune cookies.

Lo Mein-Style Pork

**Tangy Barbecue Beef**

# Tangy Barbecue Beef

**Prep:** 25 minutes  **Cook:** 10 to 12 hours on low-heat setting
**Stand:** 15 minutes  **Slow Cooker:** 3½- to 6-quart

- 2 tablespoons chili powder
- 1 teaspoon celery seeds
- ½ teaspoon salt
- ½ teaspoon freshly ground black pepper
- 1 beef brisket (about 3 pounds)
- 2 medium-size onions, thinly sliced
- 1 cup bottled smoke-flavor barbecue sauce
- ½ cup beer or ginger ale
- 8 kaiser or Portuguese rolls, split and toasted
     Leaf lettuce
     Tomato slices
     Hot-pepper sauce (optional)

1. In small bowl, combine chili powder, celery seeds, salt and pepper. Rub brisket all over with chili powder mixture. Place half of the sliced onions in 3½- to 6-quart slow cooker. Place brisket on the onions, cutting brisket to fit in slow cooker, if necessary. Place the remaining onions on top of the brisket. In small bowl, stir together barbecue sauce and beer. Pour over brisket and onions.

2. Cover slow cooker; cook on low-heat setting for 10 to 12 hours or until brisket is fork-tender.

3. Transfer brisket to cutting board, reserving sauce mixture; let brisket stand for 15 minutes. If necessary, raise temperature to high-heat setting. Halve brisket crosswise. Using two forks, pull brisket apart into shreds. Return shredded brisket to sauce mixture in slow cooker. Heat through.

4. Top bun bottoms with lettuce and tomato slices. Using a slotted spoon, spoon beef and onion mixture on top of tomato. If desired, season to taste with hot-pepper sauce. Add bun tops. Makes 8 servings.

Per serving: 404 cal., 10 g total fat (3 g sat. fat), 72 mg chol., 993 mg sodium, 44 g carbo., 3 g fiber, 31 g pro.

**SERVE-ALONG OPTIONS:** deli-style coleslaw, purchased baked beans and sliced apples and fresh pear slices served with caramel dip.

---

*Feta cheese, oregano and dried tomatoes load this meat loaf with Mediterranean flavor.*

# Mediterranean Meat Loaf

**Prep:** 20 minutes  **Cook:** 7 to 8 hours on low-heat or 3½ to 4 hours on high-heat setting  **Slow Cooker:** 3½- or 4-quart

- 1 egg
- 2 tablespoons milk
- ½ cup packaged plain dry bread crumbs
- ½ teaspoon salt
- ½ teaspoon dried oregano
- ¼ teaspoon black pepper
- 2 cloves garlic, chopped
- 1½ pounds lean ground beef (93% lean)
- ½ cup crumbled feta cheese (2 ounces)
- ¼ cup oil-pack dried tomatoes, drained and snipped
- 3 tablespoons bottled pizza or pasta sauce

1. In medium-size bowl, combine egg and milk; beat with a fork. Stir in bread crumbs, salt, oregano, pepper and garlic. Add ground beef, feta cheese and dried tomatoes; mix well. Shape meat mixture into a 5-inch round loaf.

2. Tear off an 18-inch square piece of heavy aluminum foil; cut into thirds. Fold each piece of foil into thirds lengthwise. Crisscross foil strips and place meat loaf in center of foil strips. Bringing up strips, transfer loaf and foil to a 3½- or 4-quart slow cooker (leave foil strips under meatloaf). Press loaf away from side of slow cooker. Fold strips down, leaving loaf exposed. Spread pizza sauce over loaf.

3. Cover slow cooker; cook on low-heat setting for 7 to 8 hours or on high-heat setting for 3½ to 4 hours.

4. Using foil strips, carefully lift meat loaf from slow cooker. Discard foil strips. Makes 4 to 6 servings.

Per serving: 387 cal., 18 g total fat (7 g sat. fat), 158 mg chol., 1,030 mg sodium, 14 g carbo., 1 g fiber, 40 g pro.

**SERVE-ALONG OPTIONS:** refrigerated mashed potatoes topped with grated Parmesan cheese, steamed green beans and vanilla ice cream topped with sliced bananas and hot fudge sauce.

*While this dish can be cooked on the low-heat setting, the texture and color will be better if it is cooked on the high-heat setting.*

# Asian Pepper Steak

**Prep:** 20 minutes  **Cook:** 7 hours on low-heat or 4 hours on high-heat setting  **Slow Cooker:** 6-quart

- 2 pounds beef round steak, cut against the grain into ¾-inch-thick slices
- 3 large sweet red or green peppers, seeded and cut into ¾-inch-thick slices
- 2 large onions, halved and cut into ½-inch-thick slices
- 1 can (14½ ounces) stewed tomatoes, drained
- 3 cloves garlic, chopped
- 1 cup beef broth
- ¼ cup light soy sauce
- 2 tablespoons rice wine vinegar
- 2 tablespoons cornstarch
- 1 teaspoon sugar
- 1 can (8 ounces) bamboo shoots, drained
  Hot cooked rice

**1.** Coat 6-quart slow cooker with nonstick cooking spray. Add steak; top with peppers, onions, tomatoes and garlic.

**2.** In small bowl, whisk together beef broth, soy sauce, vinegar, cornstarch and sugar. Pour over beef and vegetables. Sprinkle bamboo shoots over mixture in slow cooker.

**3.** Cover slow cooker; cook on low-heat setting for 7 hours or on high-heat setting for 4 hours. Serve with hot cooked rice. Makes 6 servings.

Per serving: 415 cal., 6 g total fat (2 g sat. fat), 86 mg chol., 851 mg sodium, 49 g carbo., 5 g fiber, 41 g pro.

**SERVE-ALONG OPTIONS:** steamed fresh snow peas and purchased pound cake served with lemon curd and fresh blueberries.

---

*Tender steak, noodles and a wonderfully rich sauce—based on cream of celery soup—make this a tempting dish for a family dinner.*

# Round Steak with Herbs

**Prep:** 15 minutes  **Cook:** 10 to 12 hours on low-heat or 5 to 6 hours on high-heat setting  **Slow Cooker:** 3½- or 4-quart

- 1 boneless beef round steak, cut ¾ inch thick (about 2 pounds)
- 1 medium-size onion, sliced
- 1 can (10¾ ounces) condensed cream of celery soup
- ½ teaspoon dried oregano
- ¼ teaspoon dried thyme
- ¼ teaspoon black pepper
- 4 cups hot cooked noodles
  Fresh oregano sprigs (optional)

**1.** Trim fat from steak. Cut steak into six serving-size pieces. Place onion in 3½- or 4-quart slow cooker; place steak pieces on onion. In small bowl, combine cream of celery soup, oregano, thyme and pepper; pour over steak.

**2.** Cover slow cooker; cook on low-heat setting for 10 to 12 hours or on high-heat setting for 5 to 6 hours.

**3.** To serve, cut steak into bite-size pieces. Toss steak and sauce with hot cooked noodles. If desired, garnish each serving with fresh oregano. Makes 6 servings.

Per serving: 392 cal., 11 g total fat (3 g sat. fat), 113 mg chol., 483 mg sodium, 32 g carbo., 2 g fiber, 39 g pro.

**SERVE-ALONG OPTIONS:** deli-style Waldorf salad and purchased lemon meringue pie.

**Round Steak with Herbs**

**Seed-Coated Pork Roast**

*A savory quintet of anise, fennel, caraway, dill and celery seeds creates a crustlike coating for this ultratender roast.*

# Seed-Coated Pork Roast

**Prep:** 30 minutes  **Cook:** 9 to 11 hours on low-heat or 4½ to 5½ hours on high-heat setting  **Slow Cooker:** 3½- to 5-quart

- 1 boneless pork shoulder roast (2½ to 3 pounds)
- 1 tablespoon soy sauce
- 2 teaspoons anise seeds, crushed
- 2 teaspoons fennel seeds, crushed
- 2 teaspoons caraway seeds, crushed
- 2 teaspoons dill seeds, crushed
- 2 teaspoons celery seeds, crushed
- ⅔ cup apple cider or apple juice
- ½ cup beef broth
- 1 tablespoon cornstarch

**1.** If necessary, cut roast to fit into 3½- to 5-quart slow cooker. Remove netting from roast, if present. Trim fat from roast. Brush soy sauce over surface of roast. On large piece of aluminum foil, combine anise seeds, fennel seeds, caraway seeds, dill seeds and celery seeds. Roll roast in seeds to coat evenly.

**2.** Place roast in the slow cooker. Pour ⅓ cup of the apple cider and the beef broth around roast.

**3.** Cover slow cooker; cook on low-heat setting for 9 to 11 hours or on high-heat setting for 4½ to 5½ hours.

**4.** Transfer roast to serving platter. For gravy, strain cooking liquid and skim off fat; transfer cooking liquid to small saucepan. In small bowl, combine the remaining ⅓ cup apple cider and the cornstarch; add to liquid in saucepan. Cook and stir until thickened and bubbly. Cook and stir for 2 minutes longer. Pass gravy with pork. Makes 8 servings.

**Per serving:** 220 cal., 9 g total fat (3 g sat. fat), 92 mg chol., 285 mg sodium, 5 g carbo., 0 g fiber, 29 g pro.

> **SERVE-ALONG OPTIONS:** mixed greens and vegetable salad, purchased hard breadsticks and purchased chocolate mousse dessert with strawberries.

*This old-fashioned pot roast will have everyone coming back for seconds.*

# Saucy Pot Roast with Noodles

**Prep:** 25 minutes  **Cook:** 10 to 12 hours on low-heat or 4 to 5 hours on high-heat setting  **Slow Cooker:** 3½- or 4-quart

- 1 beef chuck pot roast (2 to 2½ pounds)
- 1 tablespoon vegetable oil
- 2 medium-size carrots, sliced
- 2 ribs celery, sliced
- 1 medium-size onion, sliced
- 2 cloves garlic, chopped
- 1 tablespoon quick-cooking tapioca
- 1 can (14½ ounces) Italian-style stewed tomatoes
- 1 can (6 ounces) Italian-style tomato paste
- 1 tablespoon brown sugar
- ½ teaspoon salt
- ¼ teaspoon black pepper
- 1 bay leaf
  Hot cooked noodles
  Celery leaves (optional)

**1.** Trim fat from roast. If necessary, cut roast to fit into 3½- or 4-quart slow cooker. In large skillet, brown roast on all sides in hot oil.

**2.** In the slow cooker, combine carrots, celery, onion and garlic. Sprinkle tapioca over vegetables. Arrange roast to cover vegetables.

**3.** In medium-size bowl, combine tomatoes with their juices, tomato paste, brown sugar, salt, pepper and bay leaf; pour over the roast in slow cooker.

**4.** Cover slow cooker; cook on low-heat setting for 10 to 12 hours or on high-heat setting for 4 to 5 hours.

**5.** Remove and discard bay leaf. Transfer roast to cutting board, reserving cooking liquid; slice roast. Skim fat from cooking liquid. Serve beef and cooking liquid with hot cooked noodles. If desired, garnish with celery leaves. Makes 6 to 8 servings.

**Per serving:** 569 cal., 27 g total fat (10 g sat. fat), 127 mg chol., 693 mg sodium, 48 g carbo., 4 g fiber, 32 g pro.

> **SERVE-ALONG OPTIONS:** steamed fresh broccoli and purchased cherry pie topped with ice cream.

*When it comes to a down-to-earth comfort meal, it's hard to beat beef short ribs. Here, the ribs get special treatment with five-spice powder and other Asian flavorings.*

# Ginger-Orange-Glazed Short Ribs

**Prep:** 20 minutes **Cook:** 11 to 12 hours on low-heat or 5½ to 6 hours on high-heat setting **Slow Cooker:** 3½- to 5-quart

> 3 pounds beef short ribs
> 1 large red onion, cut into wedges
> 1 cup orange marmalade
> ⅓ cup water
> 2 tablespoons rice vinegar
> 1 tablespoon soy sauce
> 2 teaspoons five-spice powder
> 2 teaspoons finely chopped fresh ginger
> ½ to 1½ teaspoons chile oil
> 2 cloves garlic, chopped

**1.** Trim fat from short ribs. Set short ribs aside. Place red onion in a 3½- to 5-quart slow cooker. Add short ribs. In medium bowl, combine orange marmalade, the water, rice vinegar, soy sauce, five-spice powder, ginger, chile oil and garlic. Reserve ⅔ cup of the marmalade mixture for sauce; cover and chill. Pour the remaining marmalade mixture over ribs and onion in cooker.

**2.** Cover slow cooker; cook on low-heat setting for 11 to 12 hours or on high-heat setting for 5½ to 6 hours.

**3.** For sauce, in small saucepan, bring the reserved ⅔ cup marmalade mixture to a boil; reduce heat. Boil gently, uncovered, for 5 minutes. Remove short ribs and onion from cooker; discard cooking liquid. Serve short ribs and onion with sauce. Makes 4 to 6 servings.

**Per serving:** 452 cal., 12 g total fat (5 g sat. fat), 64 mg chol., 385 mg sodium, 58 g carbo., 1 g fiber, 29 g pro.

**SERVE-ALONG OPTIONS:** hot cooked brown rice, steamed baby carrots and purchased red velvet cupcakes.

## Slow Cooker Smarts

*Your slow cooker is great for cooking less expensive cuts of meat, such as beef short ribs. The long cooking at low heat tenderizes the meat and prevents shrinking.*

*This golden casserole is like macaroni and cheese without the macaroni. Kids will like its rosy ham, soft potatoes and rich cheese flavor.*

# Ham and Potatoes au Gratin

**Prep:** 15 minutes **Cook:** 7 to 8 hours on low-heat or 3½ to 4 hours on high-heat setting **Slow Cooker:** 3½- or 4-quart

> 2 packages (5½ ounces each) au gratin potato mix
> 2 cups diced cooked ham
> ¼ cup bottled roasted red pepper, drained and chopped
> 3 cups water
> 1 can (10¾ ounces) condensed Cheddar cheese soup
> Chopped fresh chives (optional)

**1.** Lightly coat 3½- or 4-quart slow cooker with nonstick cooking spray. Place dry au gratin potato mixes with contents of seasoning packets, the ham and roasted red pepper in the prepared slow cooker. In large bowl, stir together the water and Cheddar cheese soup. Pour over potato mixture in cooker.

**2.** Cover slow cooker; cook on low-heat setting for 7 to 8 hours or on high-heat setting for 3½ to 4 hours. If desired, sprinkle with chives. Makes 6 servings.

**Per serving:** 255 cal., 7 g total fat (3 g sat. fat), 29 mg chol., 2,087 mg sodium, 45 g carbo., 3 g fiber, 15 g pro.

**SERVE-ALONG OPTIONS:** tossed green salad, steamed baby carrots and caramel swirl ice cream served with shortbread cookies.

Ham and Potatoes au Gratin

# Poultry and Fish

**Chicken, turkey and seafood dishes go back to basics and travel the globe in this inspired chapter of tempting meals.**

Chicken and
Vegetables with Herbs

*Frozen pearl onions are an easy addition that boosts flavor. There's no need to blanch and peel them as you would fresh pearl onions.*

# Chicken and Vegetables with Herbs

**Prep:** 20 minutes  **Cook:** 7 to 8 hours on low-heat or 3½ to 4 hours on high-heat setting  **Slow Cooker:** 5½- or 6-quart

- ½ pound fresh mushrooms, halved
- I cup loose-pack frozen pearl onions
- ½ cup chicken broth
- ¼ cup dry red wine
- 2 tablespoons tomato paste
- ½ teaspoon garlic salt
- ½ teaspoon dried rosemary
- ½ teaspoon dried thyme
- ¼ teaspoon black pepper
- I bay leaf
- 4 small chicken legs (drumstick-thigh portion) (2 to 2½ pounds total), skin removed
   Chicken broth (optional)
- ¼ cup chicken broth
- 2 tablespoons all-purpose flour
   Fresh parsley sprigs (optional)

1. In 5½- or 6-quart slow cooker, combine mushrooms and pearl onions. Stir in the ½ cup chicken broth, the wine, tomato paste, garlic salt, rosemary, thyme, pepper and bay leaf. Add chicken legs to slow cooker.

2. Cover slow cooker; cook on low-heat setting for 7 to 8 hours or on high-heat setting for 3½ to 4 hours.

3. Using a slotted spoon, transfer chicken and vegetables to a serving platter. Remove and discard bay leaf. Cover chicken and vegetables and keep warm.

4. For sauce, skim fat from cooking liquid. Measure 2 cups of the cooking liquid, adding additional chicken broth, if necessary, to equal 2 cups total liquid. Transfer liquid to medium-size saucepan. In small bowl, stir the ¼ cup broth into the flour; stir into liquid in saucepan. Cook and stir until thickened and bubbly; cook and stir for 1 minute longer. Spoon some of the sauce over chicken. Pass remaining sauce. If desired, garnish with parsley. Makes 4 servings.

**Per serving:** 304 cal., 9 g total fat (2 g sat. fat), 159 mg chol., 548 mg sodium, 9 g carbo., I g fiber, 43 g pro.

**SERVE-ALONG OPTIONS:** refrigerated mashed potatoes, buttermilk biscuits, purchased fruit salad and vanilla frozen yogurt.

*A bed of colorful pasta makes the ideal backdrop for showing off this luscious creamy chicken and vegetable entrée. If you like, garnish each serving with a sprig of basil.*

# Pesto-Sauced Chicken

**Prep:** 20 minutes  **Cook:** 5 to 6 hours on low-heat or 2½ to 3 hours on high-heat setting  **Slow Cooker:** 3½- or 4-quart

- 2 pounds boneless, skinless chicken thighs, cut into I-inch pieces
- 1½ cups purchased Alfredo pasta sauce
- ¼ cup purchased basil pesto
- I package (16 ounces) frozen sweet peppers and onion stir-fry vegetables
   Hot cooked spinach linguine

1. Coat an unheated large nonstick skillet with nonstick cooking spray. Heat over medium heat. Add chicken, half at a time; cook until brown. In 3½- or 4-quart slow cooker, combine chicken, Alfredo sauce and basil pesto. Stir in frozen vegetables.

2. Cover slow cooker; cook on low-heat setting for 5 to 6 hours or on high-heat setting for 2½ to 3 hours. Serve over hot cooked linguine. Makes 6 servings.

**Per serving:** 470 cal., 20 g total fat (6 g sat. fat), 160 mg chol., 600 mg sodium, 27 g carbo., 2 g fiber, 43 g pro.

**SERVE-ALONG OPTIONS:** steamed fresh asparagus spears, sourdough rolls and French silk pie.

**Pesto-Sauced Chicken**

Chicken with
Orange Couscous

*You'll taste a hint of exotic Asian cooking from blending the sweet licorice flavor of anise seeds with the fruitiness of plums and oranges. The couscous is a snap to prepare; just stir it into boiling water about 5 minutes before dinner.*

# Chicken with Orange Couscous

**Prep:** 15 minutes  **Cook:** 5 to 6 hours on low-heat or 2½ to 3 hours on high-heat setting  **Stand:** 5 minutes
**Slow Cooker:** 3½- or 4-quart

  ¾ cup plum sauce
  ⅓ cup orange juice
  ¼ cup orange marmalade
  2 tablespoons quick-cooking tapioca
  ¼ teaspoon anise seeds, crushed
  2½ to 2¾ pounds boneless, skinless chicken thighs
  2¼ cups water
  1 tablespoon orange marmalade
  1 package (10 ounces) quick-cooking couscous
  ¼ teaspoon salt

**1.** For sauce, in small bowl, combine plum sauce, orange juice, the ¼ cup orange marmalade, the tapioca and anise seeds. Place chicken in a 3½- or 4-quart slow cooker. Pour sauce over chicken.

**2.** Cover slow cooker; cook on low-heat setting for 5 to 6 hours or on high-heat setting for 2½ to 3 hours. Remove chicken; keep warm. Skim fat from sauce.

**3.** In medium-size saucepan, combine the water and the 1 tablespoon orange marmalade; bring to a boil. Remove from heat. Stir in couscous and salt. Cover; let stand for 5 minutes. Fluff couscous with a fork just before serving. Serve chicken and sauce with couscous. Makes 6 servings.

Per serving: 538 cal., 8 g total fat (2 g sat. fat), 157 mg chol., 404 mg sodium, 70 g carbo., 3 g fiber, 44 g pro.

**SERVE-ALONG OPTIONS:** steamed fresh broccoli and brownie hot fudge sundaes.

*This classic dish is updated with green beans and mushrooms, a dash of sherry and a sprinkling of parsley. All you need is some bread and butter to round out this meal.*

# Chicken Tetrazzini

**Prep:** 20 minutes  **Cook:** 9 to 10 hours on low-heat or 4 to 5 hours on high-heat setting, plus 15 to 20 minutes on high-heat setting  **Slow Cooker:** 5- or 5½-quart

  1 medium-size onion, finely chopped
  ½ pound green beans, trimmed and cut into 1-inch pieces
  1 package (8 ounces) sliced fresh mushrooms
  6 boneless, skinless chicken thighs (about 1½ pounds total)
  1 teaspoon salt
  1 teaspoon dried thyme
  1 teaspoon black pepper
  1 can (14 ounces) chicken broth
  ½ cup cold water
  ¼ cup all-purpose flour
  ½ cup heavy cream
  1 jar (4 ounces) chopped pimientos, drained
  3 tablespoons dry sherry
  ¼ cup grated Parmesan cheese
    Hot cooked spaghetti
  1 tablespoon chopped fresh parsley (optional)

**1.** In 5- or 5½-quart slow cooker, layer chopped onion, green beans and mushrooms. Arrange chicken thighs on top. Sprinkle with salt, thyme and pepper. Pour chicken broth over all.

**2.** Cover slow cooker; cook on low-heat setting for 9 to 10 hours or on high-heat setting for 4 to 5 hours or until the chicken and green beans are tender. If necessary, raise temperature to high-heat setting.

**3.** In small bowl, combine the ½ cup cold water and flour, stirring until smooth. Add 1 cup of the cooking liquid from slow cooker to flour mixture, stirring until smooth. Stir into mixture in cooker. Cover slow cooker and cook for 10 to 15 minutes or until thickened. Stir in heavy cream, pimientos and sherry. Cover slow cooker; cook for 5 minutes longer. Stir in Parmesan cheese.

**4.** Serve chicken mixture over hot cooked spaghetti. If desired, sprinkle with parsley. Makes 6 servings.

Per serving: 505 cal., 15 g total fat (7 g sat. fat), 125 mg chol., 818 mg sodium, 55 g carbo., 5 g fiber, 35 g pro.

**SERVE-ALONG OPTIONS:** deli shredded carrot and raisin salad and cookie dough ice cream.

*Another time, use the zesty shredded chicken mixture to top quesadillas or wrap the chicken in flour tortillas.*

# Tex-Mex Chicken Tacos

**Prep:** 35 minutes  **Cook:** 4½ hours on low-heat or 3½ hours on high-heat setting, plus 10 minutes on high-heat setting
**Slow Cooker:** 5- or 5½-quart

  1  can (14½ ounces) diced tomatoes with jalapeño chiles, drained

1¼  cups salsa verde

  1  tablespoon ground cumin

  3  cloves garlic, chopped

 ½  teaspoon salt

 ½  teaspoon black pepper

  3  pounds boneless, skinless chicken thighs (10 to 12 thighs), fat removed

  1  large sweet red pepper, seeded and sliced

  1  large sweet yellow pepper, seeded and sliced

  1  medium-size onion, sliced

  1  can (14½ ounces) black beans, drained, rinsed and coarsely mashed

  1  can (14½ ounces) corn, drained

    **Tacos:**

24  hard taco shells

1½  cups shredded Monterey Jack cheese (6 ounces)

  2  avocados, halved, pitted, peeled and thinly sliced

1. In 5- or 5½-quart slow cooker, combine tomatoes, ¾ cup of the salsa verde, the cumin, garlic, salt and black pepper. Add chicken, sweet peppers and onion; stir to coat. Cover slow cooker; cook on low-heat setting for 4½ hours or on high-heat setting for 3½ hours.

2. Remove chicken from slow cooker to a cutting board and let cool slightly.

3. Strain tomato mixture over large bowl or measuring cup; set liquid aside. If necessary, raise temperature to high-heat setting. Return vegetable mixture to slow cooker; stir in black beans and corn. Cover slow cooker; cook for 10 minutes.

4. Meanwhile, using two forks, pull chicken apart into shreds. Stir shredded chicken into vegetable mixture in slow cooker. Stir in the remaining ½ cup salsa verde and 1 cup of the reserved liquid (or more if desired).

5. Tacos: Heat shells following package directions. Divide mixture evenly among shells; top each with 1 tablespoon of the cheese and 1 or 2 avocado slices. Makes 24 tacos.

Per taco: 331 cal., 4 g total fat (1 g sat. fat), 55 mg chol., 575 mg sodium, 47 g carbo., 3 g fiber, 26 g pro.

**SERVE-ALONG OPTIONS:** Mexican-style rice and vanilla ice cream served with caramel sauce and toasted chopped pecans.

*This no-fuss chicken dish is easy to put together and even easier to enjoy. Freshly grated Parmesan cheese makes it special.*

# Easy Italian Chicken

**Prep:** 20 minutes  **Cook:** 6 to 7 hours on low-heat or 3 to 3½ hours on high-heat setting  **Slow Cooker:** 3½- to 6-quart

 ½  of a medium-size head cabbage, cut into wedges (about ¾ pound)

  1  medium-size onion, sliced and separated into rings

  1  jar (4½ ounces) sliced mushrooms, drained

  2  tablespoons quick-cooking tapioca

  2  to 2½ pounds meaty chicken pieces (breast halves, thighs and drumsticks), skin removed

  2  cups purchased meatless spaghetti sauce

    Grated Parmesan cheese

    Hot cooked pasta (optional)

1. In 3½- to 6-quart slow cooker, combine cabbage wedges, onion and mushrooms. Sprinkle tapioca over vegetables. Place chicken pieces on vegetables. Pour spaghetti sauce over chicken.

2. Cover slow cooker; cook on low-heat setting for 6 to 7 hours or on high-heat setting for 3 to 3½ hours. Transfer to a serving platter. Sprinkle with Parmesan cheese. If desired, serve with hot cooked pasta. Makes 4 to 6 servings.

Per serving: 300 cal., 9 g total fat (3 g sat. fat), 94 mg chol., 662 mg sodium, 24 g carbo., 4 g fiber, 35 g pro.

**SERVE-ALONG OPTIONS:** crusty rolls or bread, mixed greens with creamy Parmesan dressing and spumoni ice cream.

Easy Italian Chicken

Turkey and
Pasta Primavera

*A sprinkling of Parmesan cheese brings a tantalizingly sharp note to this creamy blend of turkey, pasta and vegetables.*

# Turkey and Pasta Primavera

**Prep:** 20 minutes  **Cook:** 4 to 5 hours on low-heat or 2 to 2½ hours on high-heat setting  **Slow Cooker:** 4½- to 6-quart

> 2 pounds turkey breast tenderloins or boneless, skinless chicken breast halves, cut into 1-inch pieces
> 1 package (16 ounces) loose-pack frozen stir-fry vegetables (sugar snap peas, carrots, onions and mushrooms)
> 2 teaspoons dried basil, oregano or Italian seasoning
> 1 jar (16 ounces) Alfredo pasta sauce
> ¾ pound linguine or spaghetti, broken
> Shredded Parmesan cheese (optional)

**1.** In 4½- to 6-quart slow cooker, combine turkey and frozen vegetables. Sprinkle with dried herb. Stir in Alfredo sauce.

**2.** Cover slow cooker; cook on low-heat setting for 4 to 5 hours or on high-heat setting for 2 to 2½ hours.

**3.** Meanwhile, cook pasta following package directions; drain. Stir cooked pasta into mixture in slow cooker. If desired, sprinkle each serving with Parmesan cheese. Makes 8 servings.

Per serving: 488 cal., 19 g total fat (0 g sat. fat), 99 mg chol., 267 mg sodium, 39 g carbo., 3 g fiber, 37 g pro.

**SERVE-ALONG OPTIONS:** biscuits and purchased apple pie served with vanilla ice cream.

*A creamy sauce of Alfredo pasta sauce mix and herbed cream cheese cooks with mushrooms, pretty orange shredded carrots and turkey breast tenderloin pieces to top angel hair pasta. With a crisp salad, it's dinner!*

# Mushroom-Sauced Turkey

**Prep:** 30 minutes  **Cook:** 4 to 5 hours on low-heat setting  **Slow Cooker:** 4- to 5-quart

> 1 can (10¾ ounces) condensed cream of chicken soup
> ½ tub (8 ounces) cream cheese with chives and onion
> 1 package (1¼ ounces) Alfredo pasta sauce mix
> 1 can (5 ounces) evaporated milk
> ½ cup water
> 2 pounds turkey breast tenderloins, cut into ¾-inch pieces
> 2 cans (8 ounces each) sliced mushrooms, drained
> 2 cups shredded carrots
> 1 cup finely chopped onions
> Hot cooked angel hair pasta

**1.** In 4- to 5-quart slow cooker, combine cream of chicken soup, cream cheese and dry pasta sauce mix, stirring until mixed. Gradually stir in evaporated milk and the water. Add turkey, mushrooms, carrots and onions to mixture in slow cooker.

**2.** Cover slow cooker; cook on low-heat setting for 4 to 5 hours.

**3.** Serve turkey mixture over hot cooked pasta. Makes 12 servings.

Per serving: 340 cal., 9 g total fat (4 g sat. fat), 61 mg chol., 542 mg sodium, 38 g carbo., 3 g fiber, 26 g pro.

**SERVE-ALONG OPTIONS:** steamed fresh broccoli and cauliflower and custard with fruit.

## Slow Cooker Smarts

*Save time in the morning by chopping and shredding fresh vegetables the night before. Place ingredients in a tightly sealed container and refrigerate overnight.*

*Thick and chunky, this fish soup measures up to the finest chowders anywhere. If you prefer halibut or haddock, substitute either for the cod.*

# Hearty Fish Chowder

**Prep:** 25 minutes **Cook:** 6 to 7 hours on low-heat or 3 to 3½ hours on high-heat setting, plus 1 hour on high-heat setting **Slow Cooker:** 3½- or 4-quart

- 2 medium-size potatoes, chopped
- 1 cup chopped onions
- 1 can (10¾ ounces) condensed cream of celery soup
- 1 package (10 ounces) frozen whole kernel corn
- 1 package (10 ounces) frozen baby lima beans or 2 cups loose-pack frozen baby lima beans
- 1½ cups chicken broth
- ⅓ cup dry white wine or chicken broth
- 2 cloves garlic, chopped
- 1 teaspoon lemon-pepper seasoning
- 1 pound cod or other whitefish fillets
- 1 can (14½ ounces) stewed tomatoes
- ⅓ cup nonfat dry milk powder

**1.** In 3½- or 4-quart slow cooker, combine potatoes, onions, cream of celery soup, corn, lima beans, chicken broth, white wine, garlic and lemon-pepper seasoning.

**2.** Cover slow cooker; cook on low-heat setting for 6 to 7 hours or on high-heat setting for 3 to 3½ hours.

**3.** If necessary, raise temperature to high-heat setting. Place fish on the mixture in the cooker. Cover slow cooker; cook for 1 hour longer.

**4.** Add tomatoes with their juices and nonfat dry milk powder to cooker, stirring gently to break up the fish. Makes 6 servings.

**Per serving:** 310 cal., 4 g total fat (1 g sat. fat), 39 mg chol., 1,013 mg sodium, 45 g carbo., 6 g fiber, 23 g pro.

**SERVE-ALONG OPTIONS:** assorted veggies and dip, breadsticks, sorbet and sugar cookies.

*Shrimp takes on lively flavors when it's cooked in a tomato-based sauce infused with garlic and seasonings. Keep an eye on the shrimp so you don't overcook it.*

# Cajun Shrimp and Rice

**Prep:** 15 minutes **Cook:** 5 to 6 hours on low-heat or 3 to 3½ hours on high-heat setting, plus 15 minutes on high-heat setting **Slow Cooker:** 3½- or 4-quart

- 1 can (28 ounces) tomatoes, cut up
- 1 can (14 ounces) chicken broth
- 1 cup chopped onions
- 1 cup chopped green peppers
- 1 package (6 to 6¼ ounces) long-grain and wild rice mix
- ¼ cup water
- 2 cloves garlic, chopped
- ½ teaspoon Cajun seasoning
- 1 pound cooked, shelled and deveined shrimp
  Hot-pepper sauce (optional)

**1.** In 3½- or 4-quart slow cooker, combine tomatoes with their juices, chicken broth, onions, green peppers, rice mix with seasoning packet, the water, garlic and Cajun seasoning.

**2.** Cover slow cooker; cook on low-heat setting for 5 to 6 hours or on high-heat setting for 3 to 3½ hours.

**3.** If necessary, raise temperature to high-heat setting. Stir shrimp into rice mixture. Cover slow cooker; cook for 15 minutes longer. If desired, pass hot-pepper sauce. Makes 6 servings.

**Per serving:** 223 cal., 2 g total fat (0 g sat. fat), 147 mg chol., 1,063 mg sodium, 32 g carbo., 3 g fiber, 21 g pro.

**SERVE-ALONG OPTIONS:** purchased fruit salad, refrigerated cornbread twists and purchased apple pie served with vanilla ice cream.

Cajun Shrimp and Rice

# Meatless

Whether you eat meatless full time or are looking to add some vegetarian fare to a weeknight dinner, these casseroles and pastas exhibit bold, rich flavors.

Ratatouille with Parmesan Toast

*Ratatouille is a traditional French dish that typically stars eggplant, peppers, tomatoes, onions, squash, lots of garlic, herbs and olive oil. This slow-cooked version has all the classic vegetables and is made fresh with a sprinkling of fresh basil.*

# Ratatouille with Parmesan Toast

**Prep:** 30 minutes  **Cook:** 4½ to 5 hours on low-heat or 2 to 2½ hours on high-heat setting  **Broil:** 30 seconds
**Slow Cooker:** 1½-quart

**Ratatouille:**

1½ cups cubed, peeled (if desired) eggplant

½ cup coarsely chopped yellow summer squash or zucchini

½ cup coarsely chopped tomato

½ of a can (8 ounces) no-salt-added tomato sauce

⅓ cup coarsely chopped sweet red or green pepper

¼ cup finely chopped onion

¼ teaspoon salt

⅛ teaspoon black pepper

1 clove garlic, chopped

1 tablespoon chopped fresh basil

**Parmesan Toast:**

4 ½-inch-thick slices baguette-style French bread

1 teaspoon olive oil

3 tablespoons finely shredded Parmesan cheese

1. Ratatouille: In 1½-quart slow cooker, combine eggplant, squash, chopped tomato, tomato sauce, sweet pepper, onion, salt, black pepper and garlic.

2. Cover slow cooker; cook on low-heat setting for 4½ to 5 hours or on high-heat setting for 2 to 2½ hours. If no heat setting is available, cook for 4 to 4½ hours.

3. Parmesan Toast: Heat broiler. Brush one side of each bread slice with olive oil. Place bread slices, oiled sides up, on a baking sheet. Broil 3 to 4 inches from heat about 15 seconds or until toasted (watch carefully to avoid burning). Sprinkle bread slices with 1 tablespoon of the Parmesan cheese. Broil about 15 seconds longer or until cheese is melted.

4. Stir basil into mixture in cooker. Serve in shallow bowls with Parmesan Toast. Sprinkle with the remaining 2 tablespoons Parmesan cheese. Makes 2 servings.

Per serving: 248 cal., 6 g total fat (2 g sat. fat), 5 mg chol., 739 mg sodium, 39 g carbo., 6 g fiber, 10 g pro.

**SERVE-ALONG OPTIONS:** steamed green beans with almonds and purchased cheesecake.

*Toss a salad to go with this cheesy chickpea-and-veggie combo and dinner is ready.*

# Vegetable-Rice Casserole

**Prep:** 15 minutes  **Cook:** 3½ to 4½ hours on low-heat setting
**Slow Cooker:** 3½- or 4-quart

1 package (16 ounces) loose-pack frozen cauliflower, broccoli and carrots

1 can (15 ounces) chickpeas, drained and rinsed

1 can (10¾ ounces) condensed cream of celery soup or cream of mushroom soup

1 cup instant white rice

½ of a jar (15 ounces) process cheese dip (about 1 cup)

1 cup water

1. In 3½- or 4-quart slow cooker, combine frozen vegetables and chickpeas. In medium-size bowl, stir together cream of celery soup, uncooked rice, cheese dip and the water; pour over mixture in cooker.

2. Cover slow cooker; cook on low-heat setting for 3½ to 4½ hours or until vegetables and rice are tender. Stir well before serving. Makes 4 servings.

Per serving: 436 cal., 17 g total fat (10 g sat. fat), 34 mg chol., 1,923 mg sodium, 52 g carbo., 9 g fiber, 17 g pro.

**SERVE-ALONG OPTIONS:** greens salad, whole wheat rolls and raspberry sorbet.

**Slow Cooker Smarts**

*Add herbs at the right time. Because dried herbs have more staying power, crush and add them at the beginning of cooking. Add fresh herbs just minutes before serving.*

Sweet-and-Sour
Cabbage Rolls

# Sweet-and-Sour Cabbage Rolls

**Prep:** 45 minutes **Cook:** 6 to 7 hours on low-heat or 3 to 3½ hours on high-heat setting **Slow Cooker:** 5- to 6-quart

- 1 large head green cabbage
- 3½ cups purchased marinara sauce or meatless spaghetti sauce
- 1 can (15 ounces) black beans or red kidney beans, drained and rinsed
- 1 cup cooked brown rice
- ½ cup chopped carrot
- ½ cup chopped celery
- ½ cup chopped onion
- 1 clove garlic, chopped
- ⅓ cup raisins
- 3 tablespoons lemon juice
- 1 tablespoon brown sugar

**1.** Remove eight large outer leaves from cabbage. In Dutch oven, cook cabbage leaves in boiling water for 4 to 5 minutes or just until limp; drain well. Trim the heavy vein from each cabbage leaf; set leaves aside. Shred 4 cups of the remaining cabbage; place shredded cabbage in 5- to 6-quart slow cooker.

**2.** In medium-size bowl, combine ½ cup of the marinara sauce, the drained beans, cooked rice, carrot, celery, onion and garlic. Spoon about ⅓ cup of the bean mixture onto each cabbage leaf. Fold in sides; roll up each leaf.

**3.** In another medium-size bowl, combine the remaining 3 cups marinara sauce, the raisins, lemon juice and brown sugar. Stir about half of the sauce mixture into shredded cabbage in slow cooker. Place cabbage rolls on top of shredded cabbage. Spoon the remaining sauce mixture over all.

**4.** Cover slow cooker; cook on low-heat setting for 6 to 7 hours or on high-heat setting for 3 to 3½ hours. Carefully remove cabbage rolls and serve with the shredded cabbage mixture. Makes 4 servings.

*Per serving: 387 cal., 6 g total fat (1 g sat. fat), 0 mg chol., 1,368 mg sodium, 76 g carbo., 11 g fiber, 15 g pro.*

**SERVE-ALONG OPTIONS:** savory herbed muffins, tropical fruit salad and purchased carrot cake.

*With its people-pleasing combo of Cajun seasoning, black beans, tomatoes and okra, this zesty gumbo is a cut above the rest.*

# Cajun-Seasoned Vegetarian Gumbo

**Prep:** 10 minutes **Cook:** 6 to 8 hours on low-heat or 3 to 4 hours on high-heat setting **Slow Cooker:** 3½- to 4½-quart

- 2 cans (15 ounces each) black beans, drained and rinsed
- 1 can (28 ounces) diced tomatoes
- 1 package (16 ounces) frozen sweet peppers and onion stir-fry vegetables
- 2 cups loose-pack frozen cut okra
- 2 to 3 teaspoons Cajun seasoning
  Hot cooked white rice or brown rice (optional)

**1.** In 3½- to 4½-quart slow cooker, combine black beans, tomatoes with their juices, frozen stir-fry vegetables, frozen okra and Cajun seasoning.

**2.** Cover slow cooker; cook on low-heat setting for 6 to 8 hours or on high-heat setting for 3 to 4 hours. If desired, serve over hot cooked rice. Makes 6 servings.

*Per serving: 153 cal., 0 g total fat (0 g sat. fat), 0 mg chol., 639 mg sodium, 31 g carbo., 10 g fiber, 12 g pro.*

**SERVE-ALONG OPTIONS:** grilled Swiss cheese and tomato sandwiches and purchased fruit crisp.

*Enjoy these Greek-seasoned lentils on toasted pita wedges with sprinkles of sliced scallions, chopped tomatoes and a little sour cream.*

# Greek-Seasoned Lentils

**Prep:** 20 minutes **Cook:** 6 to 7 hours on low-heat or 3 to 3½ hours on high-heat setting **Slow Cooker:** 3½- to 5-quart

- 2 cups dry brown lentils, rinsed and drained
- 2 cups shredded carrots
- 1 cup chopped onions
- 3 cans (14 ounces each) vegetable broth
- 2 teaspoons Greek seasoning

**1.** Lightly coat 3½- to 5-quart slow cooker with nonstick cooking spray. In the prepared slow cooker, combine lentils, carrots, onions, vegetable broth and Greek seasoning.

**2.** Cover slow cooker; cook on low-heat setting for 6 to 7 hours or on high-heat setting for 3 to 3½ hours. Serve lentils with a slotted spoon. Makes 6 servings.

**Per serving:** 260 cal., 2 g total fat (0 g sat. fat), 0 mg chol., 874 mg sodium, 45 g carbo., 21 g fiber, 20 g pro.

**SERVE-ALONG OPTIONS:** steamed fresh cauliflower, sliced cantaloupe and angel food cake with raspberries and blueberries.

### Slow Cooker Smarts

*Avoid peeking into the pot or stirring during cooking. Because the cooker works at low temperatures, lost heat is not easily or quickly recovered.*

---

*There's no missing the meat when you have this thick, rich and varied mixture topping the pasta!*

# Pesto Beans and Pasta

**Prep:** 20 minutes **Cook:** 7 to 9 hours on low-heat or 3½ to 4½ hours on high-heat setting **Slow Cooker:** 3½- or 4-quart

- 2 cans (19 ounces each) white cannellini beans, drained and rinsed
- 1 can (14½ ounces) Italian-style stewed tomatoes
- 1 medium-size green pepper, seeded and chopped
- 1 medium-size sweet red pepper, seeded and chopped
- 1 medium-size onion, cut into thin wedges
- 2 teaspoons dried Italian seasoning
- ½ teaspoon cracked black pepper
- 4 cloves garlic, chopped
- ½ cup vegetable broth
- ½ cup dry white wine or vegetable broth
- 1 container (7 ounces) basil pesto
- ¾ pound penne pasta
- ½ cup finely shredded Parmesan cheese or Romano cheese

**1.** In 3½- or 4-quart slow cooker, combine beans, tomatoes with their juices, green pepper, sweet red pepper, onion, Italian seasoning, black pepper and garlic. Pour vegetable broth and wine over all.

**2.** Cover slow cooker; cook on low-heat setting for 7 to 9 hours or on high-heat setting for 3½ to 4½ hours. Using a slotted spoon, transfer bean mixture to a very large serving bowl, reserving cooking liquid. Stir pesto into bean mixture.

**3.** Meanwhile, cook pasta following package directions; drain well. Add pasta to bean mixture; toss gently to combine, adding enough of the reserved cooking liquid to make mixture of desired consistency. Sprinkle each serving with Parmesan cheese. Makes 6 to 8 servings.

**Per serving:** 580 cal., 20 g total fat (2 g sat. fat), 10 mg chol., 843 mg sodium, 80 g carbo., 11 g fiber, 25 g pro.

**SERVE-ALONG OPTIONS:** Mixed greens with poppy seed dressing, dinner rolls and pound cake.

Pesto Beans and Pasta

*If you like to go meatless, stock up on beans. They're hearty, filling, almost fat-free and a terrific source of fiber, protein and iron.*

# Bean and Corn Burritos

**Prep:** 20 minutes  **Cook:** 6 to 8 hours on low-heat or 3 to 4 hours on high-heat setting  **Slow Cooker:** 3½- or 4-quart

- 3 cans (15 ounces each) red kidney and/or black beans, drained and rinsed
- 1 can (14½ ounces) diced tomatoes
- 1½ cups bottled salsa or picante sauce
- 1 can (11 ounces) whole kernel corn with sweet peppers, drained
- 1 fresh jalapeño chile, seeded and finely chopped* (optional)
- 2 teaspoons chili powder
- 2 cloves garlic, chopped
- 16 (8- to 10-inch) flour tortillas, warmed**
- 2 cups shredded lettuce
- 1 cup shredded taco cheese or Cheddar cheese (4 ounces)
  Sliced scallions and/or sour cream (optional)

**1.** In 3½- or 4-quart slow cooker, combine beans, tomatoes with their juices, salsa or picante sauce, corn, jalapeño chile (if desired), chili powder and garlic.

**2.** Cover slow cooker; cook on low-heat setting for 6 to 8 hours or on high-heat setting for 3 to 4 hours.

**3.** To serve, spoon bean mixture just below centers of tortillas. Top with lettuce and cheese. If desired, top with scallions and/or sour cream. Fold bottom edge of each tortilla up and over filling. Fold in opposite sides; roll up from bottom. Makes 8 servings.

**\*Note:** Because chiles contain volatile oils that can burn your skin and eyes, avoid direct contact with them as much as possible. When working with chiles, wear plastic or rubber gloves. If your bare hands do touch the chiles, wash your hands and nails well with soap and warm water.

**\*\*Note:** To warm tortillas, heat oven to 350°. Stack tortillas and wrap tightly in aluminum foil. Warm at 350° about 10 minutes or until heated through.

Per serving: 417 cal., 5 g total fat (4 g sat. fat), 14 mg chol., 1,126 mg sodium, 69 g carbo., 12 g fiber, 17 g pro.

**SERVE-ALONG OPTIONS:** deli fruit salad, Mexican-style rice and purchased key lime pie.

*Find tubes of polenta in the produce, specialty cheese or deli sections of the supermarket.*

# Sweet Beans and Lentils over Polenta

**Prep:** 20 minutes  **Cook:** 7 to 8 hours on low-heat or 3½ to 4 hours on high-heat setting  **Slow Cooker:** 3½- or 4-quart

- 1 can (14 ounces) vegetable broth
- 1 package (12 ounces) frozen sweet soybeans (edamame)
- 1 cup dry brown lentils, rinsed and drained
- 1 medium-size sweet red pepper, seeded and chopped
- ½ cup water
- 1 teaspoon dried oregano
- 2 cloves garlic, chopped
- ½ teaspoon salt
- 1 package (16 ounces) heat-and-serve refrigerated polenta
- 2 medium-size tomatoes, chopped

**1.** In 3½- or 4-quart slow cooker, combine vegetable broth, soybeans, lentils, sweet pepper, the water, oregano, garlic and salt.

**2.** Cover slow cooker; cook on low-heat setting for 7 to 8 hours or on high-heat setting for 3½ to 4 hours.

**3.** Prepare polenta following package directions. Stir tomatoes into lentil mixture; serve over polenta. Makes 6 servings.

Per serving: 280 cal., 5 g total fat (1 g sat. fat), 0 mg chol., 794 mg sodium, 43 g carbo., 15 g fiber, 19 g pro.

**SERVE-ALONG OPTIONS:** tossed spinach and mangoes with poppy seed dressing and purchased tiramisu.

**Slow Cooker Smarts**

*To freeze a leftover meatless mixture, place it in freezer containers with tight-fitting lids. Because food expands when it freezes, leave ½ inch of headspace below the rims of the containers.*

*Herb-infused tomatoes tango with garlic, artichokes and cream—a dance that renders pasta sauce with Mediterranean flair. Garnish it with cheese and sliced olives.*

# Garlic-Artichoke Pasta

**Prep:** 15 minutes  **Cook:** 6 to 8 hours on low-heat or 3 to 4 hours on high-heat setting  **Stand:** 5 minutes
**Slow Cooker:** 3½- or 4-quart

  3  cans (14½ ounces each) diced tomatoes with basil, oregano and garlic
  2  cans (14 ounces each) artichoke hearts, drained and quartered
  6  cloves garlic, chopped
  ½  cup heavy cream
     Hot cooked linguine, fettuccine or other favorite pasta
     Sliced pimiento-stuffed green olives and/or sliced, pitted ripe olives (optional)
     Crumbled feta cheese or finely shredded Parmesan cheese (optional)

**1.** Coat 3½- or 4-quart slow cooker with nonstick cooking spray. Drain two of the cans of diced tomatoes (do not drain remaining can). In prepared slow cooker, combine drained and undrained tomatoes, artichoke hearts and garlic.

**2.** Cover slow cooker; cook on low-heat setting for 6 to 8 hours or on high-heat setting for 3 to 4 hours. Stir in heavy cream; cover the slow cooker and let stand about 5 minutes to heat through.

**3.** Serve sauce over hot cooked pasta. If desired, top with olives and/or cheese. Makes 6 servings.

Per serving: 403 cal., 8 g total fat (5 g sat. fat), 27 mg chol., 1,513 mg sodium, 68 g carbo., 7 g fiber, 13 g pro.

**SERVE-ALONG OPTIONS:** mixed greens served with Italian dressing, crusty rolls and purchased crepes, warmed and served with butter and cinnamon sugar.

*Vary the flavor of this dish by the type of curry powder you use. Because curry powder is a mix of 16 to 20 spices, each brand is different. You'll want to try a few kinds to find the one you like best.*

# Vegetable Curry

**Prep:** 25 minutes  **Cook:** 7 to 9 hours on low-heat or 3½ to 4½ hours on high-heat setting  **Stand:** 5 minutes
**Slow Cooker:** 3½- to 5-quart

  4  medium-size carrots, sliced
  2  medium-size potatoes, cut into ½-inch cubes
  1  can (15 ounces) chickpeas, drained and rinsed
  ½  pound fresh green beans, cut into 1-inch pieces
  1  cup coarsely chopped onion
  3  cloves garlic, chopped
  2  tablespoons quick-cooking tapioca
  2  teaspoons curry powder
  1  teaspoon ground coriander
  ¼  to ½ teaspoon crushed red pepper
  ¼  teaspoon salt
  ⅛  teaspoon ground cinnamon
  1  can (14 ounces) vegetable broth
  1  can (14½ ounces) diced tomatoes
     Hot cooked rice

**1.** In 3½- to 5-quart slow cooker, combine carrots, potatoes, chickpeas, green beans, onion, garlic, tapioca, curry powder, coriander, crushed red pepper, salt and cinnamon. Pour vegetable broth over all.

**2.** Cover slow cooker; cook on low-heat setting for 7 to 9 hours or on high-heat setting for 3½ to 4½ hours.

**3.** Stir in tomatoes with their juices. Cover slow cooker; let stand for 5 minutes. Serve over hot cooked rice. Makes 4 servings.

Per serving: 407 cal., 3 g total fat (0 g sat. fat), 0 mg chol., 1,068 mg sodium, 87 g carbo., 12 g fiber, 13 g pro.

**SERVE-ALONG OPTIONS:** toasted pita bread wedges and lemon sorbet topped with crushed amaretti cookies.

Vegetable Curry

# Soups and Stews

Chase away chills with irresistible meals in a bowl. Some are thick like chowders, while others feature chunks in a broth.

Chicken Stew with Potato Dumplings

*Shelf-stable, fully cooked gnocchi are your ticket to no-prep dumplings in this stick-to-your-ribs stew.*

# Chicken Stew with Potato Dumplings

**Prep:** 30 minutes  **Cook:** 6 hours on low-heat or 4 hours on high-heat setting, plus 20 to 30 minutes on high-heat setting  **Slow Cooker:** 6-quart

- 3 pounds bone-in chicken thighs, skin removed
- 2 large carrots, peeled and cut into ½-inch-thick slices
- 2 ribs celery, cut into ½-inch pieces
- 3 medium-size parsnips, peeled and cut into ½-inch-thick slices
- 1 large sweet potato (about 1 pound), peeled and cut into 1-inch cubes
- 4 scallions, trimmed and chopped
- 1 quart (4 cups) chicken broth
- 1 cup water
- ½ teaspoon dried sage leaves
- ¼ teaspoon salt
- ¼ teaspoon black pepper
- 1 package (1.1 pounds) shelf-stable, fully cooked gnocchi (dumplings)
- 2 tablespoons cornstarch mixed with ¼ cup cold water
  Hot-pepper sauce

1. Place chicken in 6-quart slow cooker. Top with carrots, celery, parsnips, sweet potato and scallions. Pour chicken broth and the water over all. Sprinkle with sage, salt and pepper.

2. Cover slow cooker; cook on low-heat setting for 6 hours or on high-heat setting for 4 hours.

3. Transfer chicken to a cutting board. If necessary, raise temperature to high-heat setting. Add gnocchi to mixture in slow cooker. Cover slow cooker; cook for 10 minutes. Meanwhile, let chicken cool slightly. Using two forks, remove chicken from bones and pull chicken apart into shreds; discard bones.

4. When gnocchi are cooked, return chicken to slow cooker. Stir cornstarch mixture into mixture in slow cooker. Cover slow cooker; cook for 10 to 20 minutes or until thickened slightly. Add hot-pepper sauce to taste before serving. Makes 8 servings.

**Per serving:** 362 cal., 10 g total fat (3 g sat. fat), 72 mg chol., 881 mg sodium, 45 g carbo., 4 g fiber, 23 g pro.

**SERVE-ALONG OPTIONS:** mixed greens served with Italian dressing and shredded Parmesan cheese and chocolate fudge cake.

*Start this quick-to-assemble recipe before you head out, and supper will be ready and waiting when you return from a busy Saturday at the game or running errands.*

# Busy-Day Beef-Vegetable Soup

**Prep:** 20 minutes  **Cook:** 8 to 10 hours on low-heat or 4 to 5 hours on high-heat setting  **Slow Cooker:** 3½- or 4-quart

- 1 pound boneless beef chuck roast, trimmed and cut into bite-size pieces
- 3 medium-size carrots, cut into ½-inch-thick slices
- 2 small potatoes, peeled (if desired) and cut into ½-inch cubes
- 1 medium-size onion, chopped
- ½ teaspoon salt
- ½ teaspoon dried thyme
- 1 bay leaf
- 2 cans (14½ ounces each) diced tomatoes
- 1 cup water
- ½ cup loose-pack frozen peas
  Fresh parsley sprigs (optional)

1. In 3½- or 4-quart slow cooker, combine beef, carrots, potatoes and onion. Sprinkle with salt and thyme. Add bay leaf. Add tomatoes with their juices and the water.

2. Cover slow cooker; cook on low-heat setting for 8 to 10 hours or on high-heat setting for 4 to 5 hours. Remove and discard bay leaf. Stir in frozen peas. If desired, garnish with parsley. Makes 4 servings.

**Per serving:** 269 cal., 4 g total fat (1 g sat. fat), 67 mg chol., 746 mg sodium, 29 g carbo., 4 g fiber, 28 g pro.

**SERVE-ALONG OPTIONS:** crusty bread and apple slices served with purchased caramel dip.

Busy-Day Beef-Vegetable Soup

Wild Rice and Chicken Soup

*Cream of chicken soup, cooked chicken and chicken broth triple the poultry flavor of this no-fuss, hearty soup.*

# Wild Rice and Chicken Soup

**Prep:** 20 minutes  **Cook:** 6 to 8 hours on low-heat or 3 to 4 hours on high-heat setting  **Slow Cooker:** 5- to 6-quart

  2½  cups chopped cooked chicken
    2  cups sliced fresh mushrooms
    2  medium-size carrots, coarsely shredded
    2  ribs celery, sliced
    1  can (10¾ ounces) condensed cream of chicken soup or cream of mushroom soup
    1  package (6 ounces) long-grain and wild rice mix
    5  cups chicken broth
    5  cups water

1. In 5- to 6-quart slow cooker, combine cooked chicken, mushrooms, carrots, celery, cream of chicken soup, rice and the contents of the rice seasoning packet. Gradually stir in chicken broth and the water.

2. Cover slow cooker; cook on low-heat setting for 6 to 8 hours or on high-heat setting for 3 to 4 hours. Makes 8 to 10 servings.

Per serving: 221 cal., 7 g total fat (2 g sat. fat), 44 mg chol., 1,251 mg sodium, 23 g carbo., 2 g fiber, 18 g pro.

**SERVE-ALONG OPTIONS:** grilled cheese sandwiches and purchased frosted sugar cookies.

*This zesty stick-to-the-ribs soup boasts six seasonings plus Italian sausage. Vary the spiciness by choosing either sweet or hot sausage.*

# "It's Italian" Sausage Soup

**Prep:** 30 minutes  **Cook:** 8 to 10 hours on low-heat or 4 to 5 hours on high-heat setting, plus 20 minutes on high-heat setting  **Slow Cooker:** 4½- to 6-quart

    1  pound Italian sausage (remove casings, if present)
    1  large onion, chopped
    1  clove garlic, chopped
    2  medium-size carrots, chopped
    1  rib celery, chopped
    1  can (14½ ounces) diced tomatoes
    1  can (8 ounces) tomato sauce
    1  teaspoon dried oregano
  ½  teaspoon dried rosemary
  ½  teaspoon dried basil
  ¼  teaspoon dried thyme
  ¼  teaspoon fennel seeds
    1  bay leaf
    3  cans (14 ounces each) reduced-sodium chicken broth
  ½  cup orzo pasta or finely broken capellini pasta
       Finely shredded Parmesan cheese (optional)

1. In large skillet, combine Italian sausage, onion and garlic. Cook over medium heat until sausage is cooked through, stirring to break into bite-size pieces. Drain off fat.

2. In 4½- to 6-quart slow cooker, combine carrots and celery. Place sausage mixture on top of vegetables. In medium-size bowl, combine tomatoes with their juices, tomato sauce, oregano, rosemary, basil, thyme, fennel seeds and bay leaf. Pour over sausage mixture. Pour chicken broth over.

3. Cover slow cooker; cook on low-heat setting for 8 to 10 hours or on high-heat setting for 4 to 5 hours.

4. If necessary, raise temperature to high-heat setting. Stir in pasta. Cover slow cooker; cook for 20 minutes longer. Remove and discard bay leaf. If desired, serve with Parmesan cheese. Makes 8 servings.

Per serving: 250 cal., 13 g total fat (5 g sat. fat), 38 mg chol., 923 mg sodium, 17 g carbo., 2 g fiber, 12 g pro.

**SERVE-ALONG OPTIONS:** deli antipasto platter, breadsticks and shortcakes with fruit and whipped topping.

*Evaporated milk is used in this chowder because it adds creamy richness and, unlike regular milk, it won't break down during the slow cooking time.*

# Swiss, Ham and Broccoli Chowder

**Prep:** 15 minutes **Cook:** 6 to 7 hours on low-heat or 3 to 3½ hours on high-heat setting, plus 30 minutes on high-heat setting **Slow Cooker:** 3½- or 4-quart

    2 cans (10¾ ounces each) condensed cream of celery soup
    1 can (12 ounces) evaporated milk
    ½ cup water
    1 package (16 to 20 ounces) refrigerated diced potatoes or 3 cups loose-pack frozen diced hash brown potatoes with onion and peppers, thawed
    2 cups diced cooked ham
    2 ribs celery, finely chopped
    8 ounces process Swiss cheese slices, torn into small pieces
    2 cups chopped fresh broccoli or loose-pack frozen chopped broccoli, thawed

**1.** In 3½- or 4-quart slow cooker, combine cream of celery soup, evaporated milk and the water. Gently stir potatoes, ham and celery into mixture in slow cooker.

**2.** Cover slow cooker; cook on low-heat setting for 6 to 7 hours or on high-heat setting for 3 to 3½ hours.

**3.** If necessary, raise temperature to high-heat setting. Stir in Swiss cheese and broccoli. Cover slow cooker; cook for 30 minutes longer. Makes 6 servings.

**Per serving:** 460 cal., 24 g total fat (13 g sat. fat), 78 mg chol., 2,148 mg sodium, 34 g carbo., 4 g fiber, 24 g pro.

**SERVE-ALONG OPTIONS:** whole wheat bread slices served with butter and purchased apple cake served with caramel-swirl ice cream.

## Slow Cooker Smarts

*It's OK to brown sausage or ground meat and refrigerate overnight to add to the slow cooker the next morning. Browning fully cooks ground meat.*

*Because the meatballs are cooked before they're frozen, you can add them straight from the package to the slow cooker.*

# Meatball-Vegetable Stew

**Prep:** 10 minutes **Cook:** 6 to 8 hours on low-heat or 3 to 4 hours on high-heat setting **Slow Cooker:** 3½- or 4-quart

    1 package (16 or 18 ounces) frozen cooked meatballs
    1 package (16 ounces) loose-pack frozen mixed vegetables
    1 can (14½ ounces) diced tomatoes with onion and garlic or stewed tomatoes
    1 jar (12 ounces) mushroom gravy
    ⅓ cup water
    1½ teaspoons dried basil

**1.** In 3½- or 4-quart slow cooker, combine cooked meatballs and mixed vegetables. In medium-size bowl, stir together tomatoes with their juices, gravy, the water and basil. Pour over meatballs and vegetables.

**2.** Cover slow cooker; cook on low-heat setting for 6 to 8 hours or on high-heat setting for 3 to 4 hours. Makes 4 servings.

**Per serving:** 472 cal., 32 g total fat (14 g sat. fat), 87 mg chol., 1,833 mg sodium, 26 g carbo., 6 g fiber, 21 g pro.

**SERVE-ALONG OPTIONS:** assorted relishes, baguette-style French bread served with butter and purchased pumpkin bars with lemon cream frosting.

Meatball-Vegetable Stew

Chicken
Tortilla Soup

*There's no need to measure herbs or spices
for this soup. They're already in the seasoned
chicken broth and Mexican-style tomatoes.*

# Chicken Tortilla Soup

**Prep:** 15 minutes  **Cook:** 6 to 7 hours on low-heat or 3 to
3½ hours on high-heat setting  **Slow Cooker:** 3½- or 4-quart

 2  cans (14 ounces each) chicken broth with roasted garlic
 1  can (14½ ounces) Mexican-style stewed tomatoes
 2  cups shredded cooked chicken
 2  cups loose-pack frozen sweet peppers and onion stir-fry
    vegetables
 1  cup tortilla chips
    Sliced fresh jalapeño chiles* (optional)

**1.** In 3½- or 4-quart slow cooker, combine chicken broth,
tomatoes with their juices, chicken and frozen vegetables.

**2.** Cover slow cooker; cook on low-heat setting for 6 to 7 hours
or on high-heat setting for 3 to 3½ hours.

**3.** To serve, ladle soup into warm soup bowls and top with
tortilla chips. If desired, top with chiles. Makes 4 servings.

**\*Note:** Because chiles contain volatile oils that can burn your
skin and eyes, avoid direct contact with them as much as
possible. When working with chiles, wear plastic or rubber
gloves. If your bare hands do touch the chiles, wash your
hands and nails well with soap and warm water.

Per serving: 181 cal., 4 g total fat (1 g sat. fat), 36 mg chol., 1,383 mg sodium, 19 g carbo.,
1 g fiber, 18 g pro.

**SERVE-ALONG OPTIONS:** fresh fruit plate and cheesecake with cherry sauce.

---

*Yellow split peas add an autumnal hue. During
cooking, the peas soften and begin to fall apart,
which helps bring a pleasing—but not overly
thick—consistency to the cozy soup.*

# Golden Turkey-Split Pea Soup

**Prep:** 20 minutes  **Cook:** 9 to 10 hours on low-heat or 4½ to
5 hours on high-heat setting  **Slow Cooker:** 4½- or 5-quart

 2  cups dry yellow split peas
 2  cans (14 ounces each) reduced-sodium chicken broth
 2  cups water
 2  cups loose-pack frozen whole kernel corn
 1½ cups sliced carrots
 1  can (10¾ ounces) condensed cream of chicken soup
 ½  pound cooked smoked turkey sausage, halved lengthwise and
    sliced
 ½  cup sliced scallions
 ½  cup chopped sweet red pepper
 2  teaspoons dried thyme

**1.** Rinse and drain split peas. In 4½- or 5-quart slow cooker,
combine split peas, chicken broth, the water, frozen corn,
carrots, cream of chicken soup, turkey sausage, scallions,
sweet pepper and thyme.

**2.** Cover slow cooker; cook on low-heat setting for 9 to 10 hours
or on high-heat setting for 4½ to 5 hours. Makes 6 servings.

Per serving: 409 cal., 8 g total fat (2 g sat. fat), 30 mg chol., 1,076 mg sodium, 60 g carbo.,
19 g fiber, 27 g pro.

**SERVE-ALONG OPTIONS:** deli fruit salad, soft breadsticks
and purchased graham cracker tart crusts filled with
canned lemon pie filling and topped with whipped cream.

**Slow Cooker Smarts**

*It may be tempting to
brown stew meat the night
before just as you would
ground meat. However,
because browning doesn't
completely cook stew
meat, you'll need to
complete this step just
before plugging in your
slow cooker.*